Reading Wor
Everyday Wo

LEVEL 4

Abiyoyo

George Murphy
Series Editor – Jean Conteh

MACMILLAN

About this Book

To the Teacher or Parent

This book tells the story of three boys who decide to take a short cut home from school. Both boys and girls will enjoy the story, even though the main characters are three boys. It is an imaginary story. We are left with the question at the end of what 'Abiyoyo' really is.

Children often feel frightened of things they do not understand. Stories like 'Abiyoyo' can help them to overcome their fears. Because the story has a humorous element, they can see that their fears are usually not as bad as they seem.

The book is designed for children to read on their own. The simple language will make it fun and easy for them to read. The pictures will help them understand the words.

Use the book like this:

- Before you give the book to children to read, see if they can read the title, look at the picture on the cover and tell you what the story will be about.

- Ask the children if they can guess what Abiyoyo could be. Is it a real animal or a monster?

- Let the children read the book by themselves. When they finish, ask if they enjoyed it.

- Let children look on page 28–31, where there are some questions and activities to help them understand and enjoy the story better.

Above all, let children enjoy reading the book. This will help them become interested in reading. They will want to learn to read for themselves, and become independent readers.

Tika, Brima and Daniel were walking home from school. It was very hot. The journey along the dusty road was very long. They felt very tired.

They came to a short cut. A path curved through the long, brown grasses. The path went past a baobab tree. There were some rocks beyond the tree.

Some people said Abiyoyo the monster lived in a cave in the rocks.

Daniel was hot and tired. He wanted to take the short cut. He was frightened of Abiyoyo, but he thought he might be brave if his friends came with him.

'It's too hot to walk home this way,' said Daniel. 'Let's take the short cut past the baobab tree.'

'Abiyoyo the monster lives in the cave next to the baobab tree,' Tika said.

'My sister says Abiyoyo has horns as sharp as a knife.'

'My brother says Abiyoyo's roar is as loud as a lion's,' said Brima.

'My sister says Abiyoyo eats a lot of little boys,' said Daniel. 'So his belly is as big as the drum they play on Festival day.'

Daniel tried to be brave.

'I don't believe in Abiyoyo,' he said. 'Come with me past the baobab tree. We will get home quickly.'

Tika and Brima whispered to each other.
'We will go with you past the baobab tree, if you make us a promise,' Brima said to Daniel.
'What is the promise?' asked Daniel.
'We want you to go up right up to the mouth of Abiyoyo's cave,' said Tika.
'Yes, right up to the mouth of the cave,' agreed Brima. 'Then we want you to shout, "Abiyoyo, Abiyoyo, I'm not afraid of you!" Then we will know if there really is an Abiyoyo.'

Tika and Brima thought Daniel would not agree to their challenge. But Daniel was too proud to admit his fear.

'I agree to your challenge,' Daniel said. 'But you two must be one step behind me when I get to the cave.'

Tika and Brima whispered to each other. Daniel hoped they would not agree to his challenge. But they were as proud as he was!

'We will come with you to the mouth of the cave,' Brima said. 'We will shout, "Abiyoyo, Abiyoyo, we're not afraid of you!" We will do as you say and we will stand only one step behind you.'

The boys all shook hands to show they would keep their word.

They left the dusty road. They walked through the tall brown grasses of the bush. They walked very slowly. They followed the narrow path beside the dried-up river. They walked very, very slowly.

At last, they came to the baobab tree. The rocks were beyond the tree. In the centre of the rocks was the dark entrance to a cave.

'If you don't want to go up to the cave, we will understand,' Tika said to Daniel.

'We can creep past the cave. We will never tell anyone how frightened you were.'

'I want to go up to the cave!' said Daniel. 'If you two are frightened, I will understand. You can creep past the cave. I will never tell anyone how frightened you were.'

'Don't worry about us,' Brima said. 'We're not frightened of Abiyoyo. We agreed to stay one step behind you, and we will.'

So the three boys walked up the twisting track that led to Abiyoyo's cave.

In front of the cave was a wide, dusty ledge. The boys stood on the ledge. They looked into the darkness. At last, Daniel stepped forward.

'Abiyoyo! Abiyoyo! Great horned Abiyoyo!' shouted Daniel. 'Are you alive or dead?'

No answer came from the cave.

'Then we'll take one step, two steps, three steps. We're not afraid!' said Daniel.

He took three large steps into the mouth of the cave. Tika and Brima followed.

'Abiyoyo! Abiyoyo! Loud roaring Abiyoyo!' said Daniel, more nervously and quietly. 'Are you alive or dead?'

Again, no reply came from the cave.

'Then we'll take one step, two steps, three steps. We're not afraid!' said Daniel.

Daniel took three steps towards the cave. Tika and Brima followed.

Now they were almost inside the cave. Daniel wanted to turn and run home as fast as he could, but his friends were right behind him.

Daniel whispered, 'Abiyoyo! Abiyoyo! Drum-bellied Abiyoyo! Are you alive or dead?'

There was still no sound from the darkness.

'Then we'll tiptoe one step, tiptoe two steps, tiptoe three steps. We're not afraid!' Daniel said.

So Daniel tiptoed forward, until the fierce heat of the sun was no longer beating on his head. Tika and Brima also crept into the cave.

For a moment, all they could see were the dark shadows at the back of the cave. Then they saw two horrible monster horns. Then they saw a horrible monster belly. Then they heard a horrible monster roar.
'GRRRRRRRRRR!!!'

Tika and Brima and Daniel turned and ran as fast as they could. They ran over the dusty ledge. They ran down the twisting track.

They ran past the baobab tree. They ran along the narrow path beside the dried-up river.

They ran through the tall brown grasses of the bush. They ran until they got to the dusty road.

They looked back, but they could not see Abiyoyo. All they could see was a cow. It was rubbing its head against the trunk of the baobab tree.

'Abiyoyo will eat that cow before night falls,' said Daniel.

They set off again along the dusty road. It was cooler now. The sun had started to sink towards the horizon.

Then they heard a shout. Daniel's father was waving to them. They ran to meet him.

'Where have you been?' he asked. 'You are late. I was worried. Did you take the short cut past the baobab tree? There are dangerous creatures around that place. They go looking for water in the dried up stream. They take shelter in that cave over there.'

The three friends did not tell Daniel's father about Abiyoyo. They did not mention their adventure in the monster's cave.

Yet, later that night, the boys told their tale to their younger brothers and sisters. They told them they had seen Abiyoyo in his cave. And each told about how brave he had been.

Daniel told his little sister about the monster's great sharp horns. He told her about the monster's roar as loud as a lion's. He told her about the monster's belly, as big as a bass drum from eating little boys and girls.

Activity Page

1. Why do you think the boys did not tell Daniel's father about Abiyoyo? What do you think his father would have said to them if they had told him?

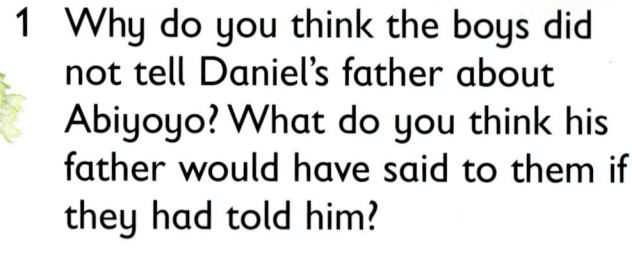

2. What do you think Abiyoyo really is? What do you think Abiyoyo looks like?

3. Do you think that the boys were right to be frightened of Abiyoyo? Write a few sentences about a time when you were frightened. Explain why you were frightened and what happened.

4 List the ways that Abiyoyo is described in the story. Draw a picture of what you think Abiyoyo looks like.

5 On page 7, it says that Abiyoyo's roar was as loud as a lion's. This is called a 'simile'. It shows us how one thing is similar to another. Can you find any other similes in the story? Look on pages 6 and 8. Write them down.

6 Make a list of similes that you know, and make up some more of your own.

Activity page

Activity page

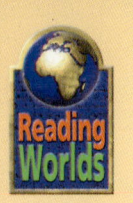

7 Here are six sentences that tell us some of the things that happened in the story. Can you put them in the correct order?

> The boy saw a cow outside the cave where the monster lived.
>
> The boys told their brothers and sisters about the monster
>
> Tika and Brima made Daniel promise to go into the cave.
>
> The monster roared at the boys.
>
> The boys went into the cave and shouted to the monster.
>
> The boys ran away from the monster.

Activity page

8   With your friends, make up a play about the story of Abiyoyo. Decide who will take the parts of Tika, Daniel, Brima, Daniel's father and his little sister. How will you represent Abiyoyo in the play?
   When you are ready, ask your teacher if you can perform your play for the rest of your class.

31

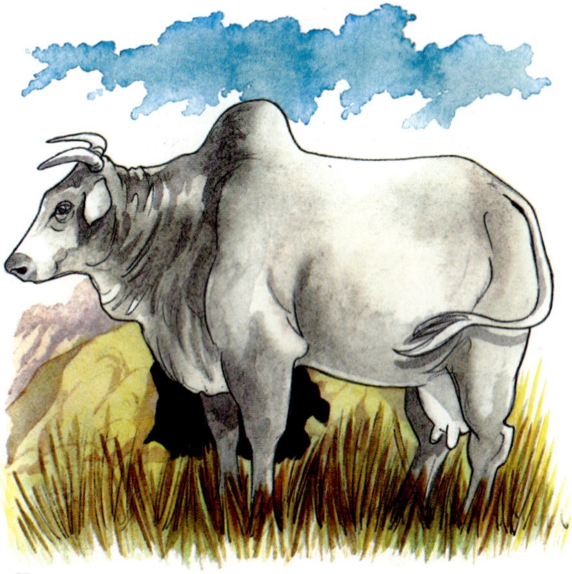